LEARN THE ESSENTIAL CHORDS YOU NEED TO START PLAYING ROCK NOW!

DVD VIDEO INCLUDED

ROCK GUITAR CHORDS

BY CHAD JOHNSON

D0613487

ISBN 978-1-4584-0030-7

HAL•LEONARD®
CORPORATION

7777 W. BLUEMOUND RD. P.O. BOX 13819 MILWAUKEE, WI 53213

In Australia Contact:
Hal Leonard Australia Pty. Ltd.
4 Lentara Court
Cheltenham, Victoria, 3192 Australia
Email: ausadmin@halleonard.com.au

Visit Hal Leonard Online at
www.halleonard.com

Introduction

Welcome to *Rock Guitar Chords*. This book will teach you the chords you must know if you want to play rock. The aim is to get you jamming quickly, so we won't get bogged down in too many details. This is not a comprehensive method. Rather, it concentrates on the chord shapes that have stood the test of time and appear in countless songs throughout rock's history.

You'll find that some of these chords will sound best with some good distortion (like power chords), whereas others may work best with a cleaner sound. However, feel free to experiment in this regard. After all, guitar players wouldn't have even discovered distortion in the first place if it weren't for experimentation! So grab your guitar and let's get to rockin'.

About the DVD

The DVD that accompanies this book is a powerful teaching tool. It contains audio/visual examples of every chord covered. The chords are first strummed and then plucked string-by-string, so you can hear each individual note and make sure you've got it right. Also, each chord progression is demonstrated with a full band accompaniment so you can hear these chords in the proper context. Tuning notes are also included on the DVD.

Chord grids are provided for many of the examples in the book—especially after a chord type is first introduced—but eventually you'll figure out where they are on your own. The neck diagram in the Appendix will be your guide here, but also remember that you can see every chord form used in each example on the DVD as well.

Table of Contents

How to Read Chord Diagrams 4

A Brief Chord Theory Primer 4

POWER CHORDS 5

OPEN CHORDS 10

BARRE CHORDS .14

SEVENTH CHORDS 19

OTHER CHORD TYPES 25

SONG EXAMPLES 29

Appendix 32

How to Read Chord Diagrams

The chords in this book are presented in chord diagram (or chord grid) fashion. The six vertical lines represent the strings; the lowest pitched (thickest) string is on the left, and the highest pitched (thinnest) is on the right.

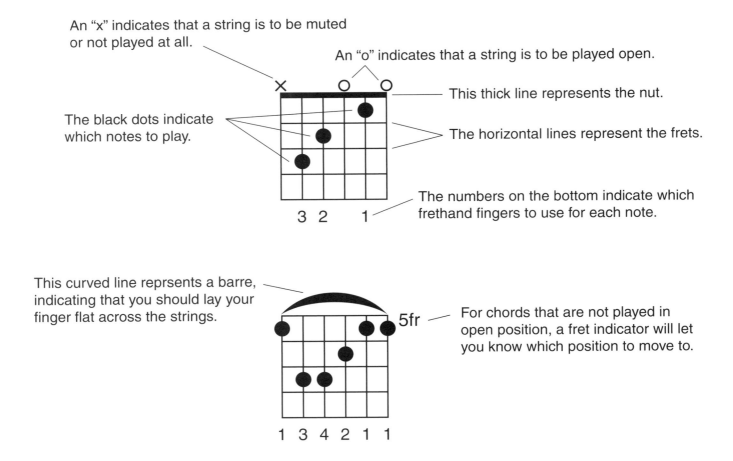

An "x" indicates that a string is to be muted or not played at all.

An "o" indicates that a string is to be played open.

This thick line represents the nut.

The black dots indicate which notes to play.

The horizontal lines represent the frets.

The numbers on the bottom indicate which frethand fingers to use for each note.

This curved line reprsents a barre, indicating that you should lay your finger flat across the strings.

For chords that are not played in open position, a fret indicator will let you know which position to move to.

A Brief Chord Theory Primer

Chords are built from intervals, or degrees, of notes from a major (or minor) scale. A major scale contains seven notes, and those notes are numbered 1 through 7. (The 1 is also commonly referred to as the "root" or "tonic.") So if a chord contains the root, 3rd, and 5th, then it contains the 1st, 3rd, and 5th notes of the root's major scale. If it contains a root, ♭3rd, and 5th, then the 3rd is lowered by a half step. This is referred to as a chord's formula. The formula for each type of chord in this book is given.

In order to understand how the chords in this book are built, you simply need to know all twelve major scales, which are found in the Appendix, and apply the formula to a particular root note.

For example, the formula for a major chord is root, 3rd, 5th (or 1–3–5). If you want to understand how a C major chord is built, you would look in the Appendix to find the C major scale. Its notes are C–D–E–F–G–A–B (no sharps or flats). Take the 1st (C), 3rd (E), and 5th (G) notes, and you have the chord. A C major chord is spelled C–E–G.

The formula for a minor chord is 1–♭3–5. So, to build a Cm chord, you would only have to lower the 3rd note (E) down a half step to E♭. So a Cm chord is spelled C–E♭–G. You can use this method to determine the spelling of any chord presented in this book.

A power chord is possibly the most common type of rock chord. It's a two-note chord comprised of a root and a 5th, so its formula is 1–5. You can play a power chord two different ways: as an *open-string form*, or as a *moveable form*.

Open-String Power Chords

An *open-string chord* (or just open chord) is a chord that contains at least one open string. Let's check out your first power chord: E5.

E5

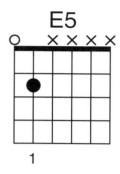

If you move everything over one string, you get an A5 chord. Be sure to avoid picking the low E string.

A5

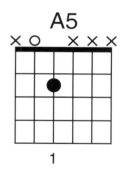

Repeating that process one more time will give us a D5 chord.

D5

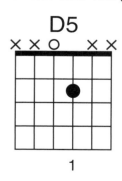

Now let's hear what these chords sound like in action. When we play a series of chords, as in a song, we're playing a *chord progression*.

Example 1

In this next example, try using the *palm mute* technique. As you pick, lay your palm on the strings where they meet the bridge. You'll get a choked, muffled sound.

Example 2

It's also very common to double the root an octave higher in power chords. Here's what you get when you do that with these forms. You'll need to *barre* (lay flat) your first finger for the E5 and A5 chords, so take care to strum only the strings indicated.

E5

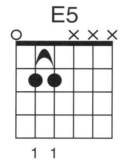

A5

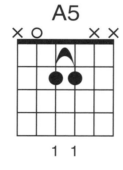

D5

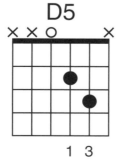

We'll use these three-string forms in this next example, where we're mixing chord strums with rests (beats of silence) to achieve a big, dramatic sound. For the rests, touch the strings in between strums to quiet them.

Example 3

You don't always have to strum these chords either. You can also pluck through the notes individually, which is called an *arpeggio*. Here's what the same chord progression sounds like when we arpeggiate the chords.

Example 4

You can also create a nice texture by leaving lots of space, as in this next example.

Example 5

Moveable Power Chords

A *moveable chord* is one that doesn't contain any open strings. They're called moveable because you can slide them anywhere on the neck to play the chord from a different root. There are two main forms commonly used for moveable power chords: the 6th-string form and the 5th-string form.

6th-String Form

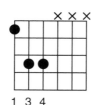

1 3 4

5th-String Form

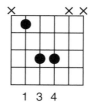

1 3 4

If you play the 6th-string form with your first finger on the third fret, you have a G5 chord.

G5

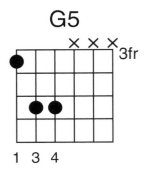

If you play the 5th-string form with your first finger on the third fret, you have a C5 chord.

C5

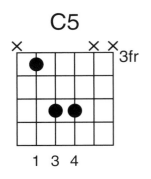

You can move these forms anywhere along either one of these strings to play different chords. (Refer to the neck diagram in the Appendix for the names of all the notes on the fretboard.)

Example 6

Now let's try mixing these two new chords with our open power chords.

Example 7

In this example, listen for the *scratch rhythm technique.* It's accomplished by laying your frethand fingers lightly on the strings to mute them (but not pushing down) and strumming to create a percussive effect. You'll get some practice changing between chords quickly in this one.

Example 8

Again, you commonly see these moveable forms in their two-string versions as well.

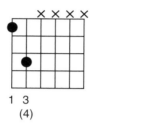
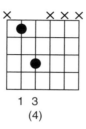

Here we're going to focus on open chords, or *triads*, instead of just power chords. Triads are made up of three notes: a root, a 3rd, and 5th. Because they have a 3rd, these chords can either be major or minor, as opposed to power chords, which are neither (because they lack a 3rd).

The formula for a major chord is 1–3–5; a minor chord's formula is 1–♭3–5.

Major Chords

Here's our first major chord: E major.

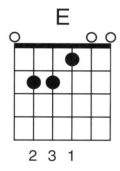

And here's A major.

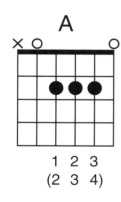

Note that when a chord name consists of only a capital letter (such as E or A), it's implied that it's a major chord.

These chords aren't often used with loads of distortion the way power chords are. They usually sound best with a clean tone or a half dirty tone.

Example 9

Let's learn a few more open major chords.

D

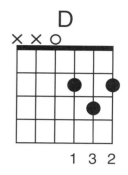

G

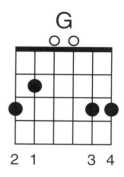

C

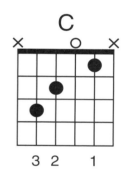

Example 10

In this example, listen to how each chord is palm-muted at first and then allowed to ring out.

Example 11

Here we're arpeggiating through the chords with a shuffle feel. This gives the notes a lopsided feel. Think of a blues song like "Pride and Joy" or "Tore Down," and you're hearing a shuffle feel. (On the E chord, we're only playing the top four strings.)

Example 12

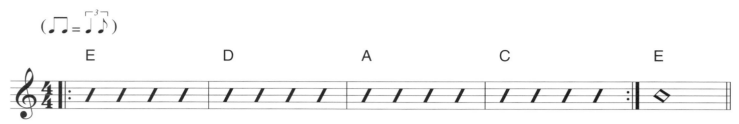

Minor Chords

Now let's look at some minor chords. These have a dark, sad quality compared to a major chord's bright, happy sound.

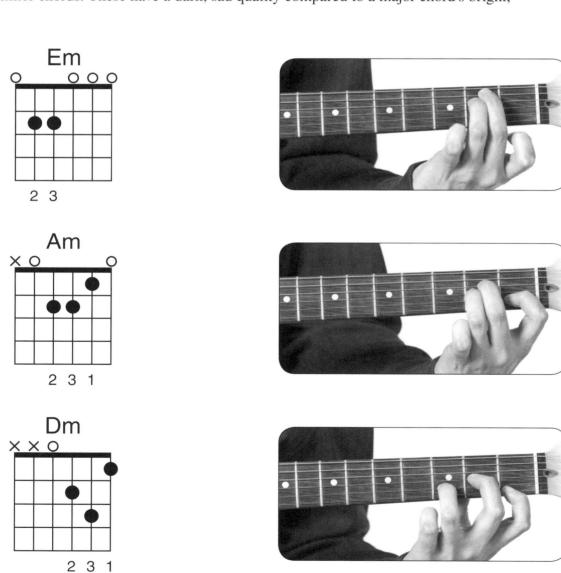

A chord symbol for a minor chord contains the suffix "m" after the capital letter.

Notice that each one of these chords differs from the same major chord by only one note. That note is the chord's 3rd. Remember: minor chords are the same as major, except the 3rd is flatted (lowered by a half step).

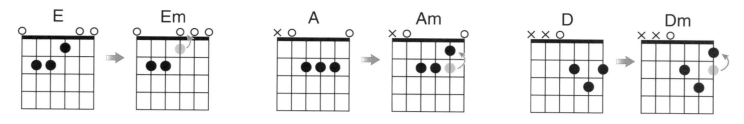

Example 13

This next example is in 12/8, which means four "beats" counted in groups of three, like this:

1 2 3, **4** 5 6, **7** 8 9, **10** 11 12.

Example 14

Most songs are made up of combinations of major and minor chords.

Example 15

Example 16

Barre chords are usually the most difficult to master, because they require the most hand strength. There are two main barre chord forms commonly used: the 6th-string form and the 5th-string form.

Major Barre Chords

6th-String Form

Here, you'll be barring across all six strings with your first finger. This is sometimes called an "E-form" because it resembles an open E chord.

5th-String Form

In this form, you're barring across three strings with your third finger. This is sometimes called an "A-form" because it resembles an open A chord.

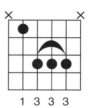

If you play the 6th-string form with your first finger on the third fret, you have a G chord.

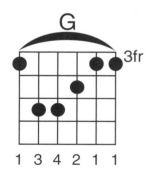

If you play the 5th-string form with your first finger on the third fret, you have a C chord.

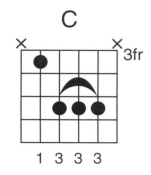

Again, as with the moveable power chord shapes, you can move these forms anywhere along either one of these strings to play different chords. (Refer to the neck diagram in the Appendix for the names of all the notes on the fretboard.)

This example uses all 6th-string forms.

Example 17

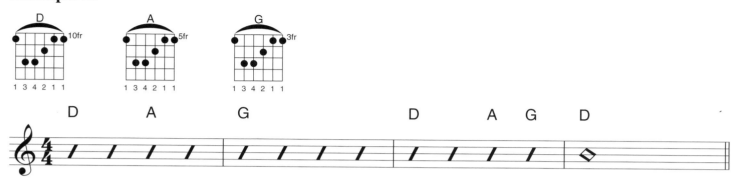

And here we're moving only the 5th-string form around.

Example 18

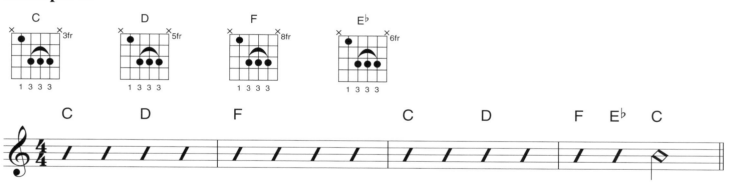

Now let's combine the forms.

Example 19

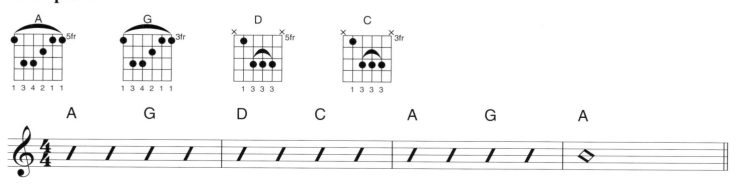

Minor Barre Chords

As with the open chords, the minor barre chords differ only from the major ones by one note.

6th-String Form

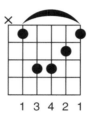

1 3 4 1 1 1

5th-String Form

This is slightly different than its major counterpart; here, you're barring five strings with your first finger.

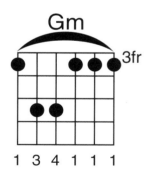

1 3 4 2 1

Again, you'll see these referred to as E-forms and A-forms, respectively. If you play the 6th-string form with your first finger on the third fret, you have a Gm chord.

Gm

3fr

1 3 4 1 1 1

If you play the 5th-string form with your first finger on the third fret, you have a Cm chord.

Cm

3fr

1 3 4 2 1

Let's move around the 6th-string form for this example.

Example 20

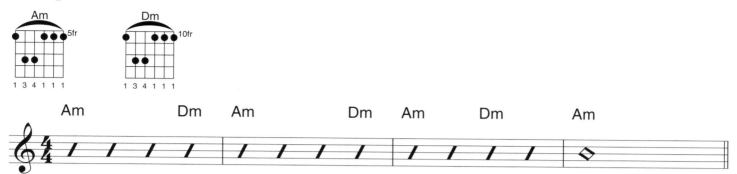

This one uses the 5th-string form.

Example 21

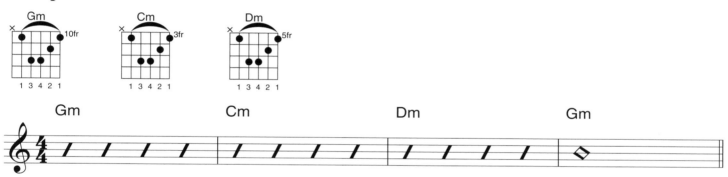

And now we'll combine both forms.

Example 22

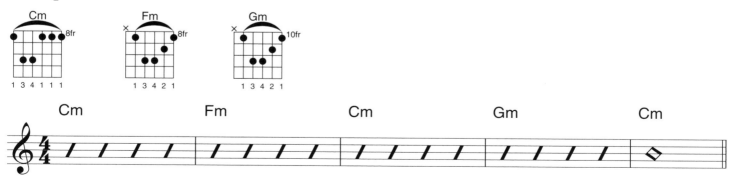

Now let's combine our major and minor barre chord shapes in both forms.

Example 23

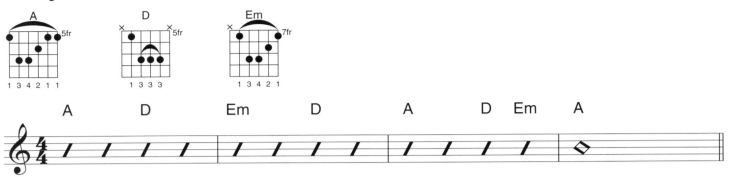

Example 24

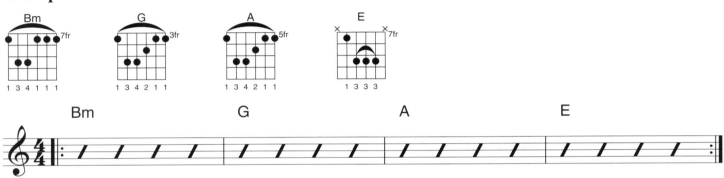

Example 25

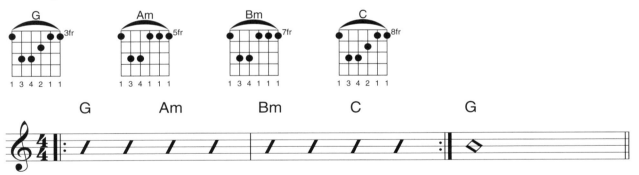

Example 26

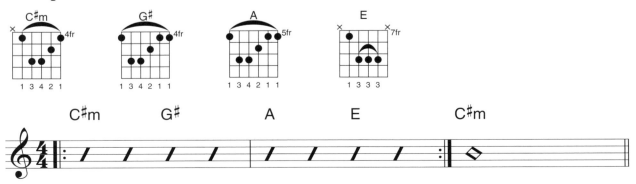

SEVENTH CHORDS

A *seventh chord* has four different notes: a root, 3rd, 5th, and 7th. There are many different types, but we'll look at the two most commonly found in rock: the dominant 7th (1–3–5–♭7) and the minor 7th (1–♭3–5–♭7).

Dominant Seventh Chords

Dominant seventh chords sound bluesy and funky. They contain a major 3rd like a major chord, but the ♭7th makes them sound less stable and a bit tougher.

Open Forms

E7

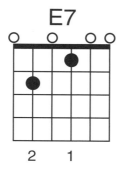

2 1

A7

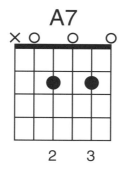

2 3

D7

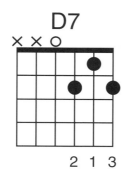

2 1 3

G7

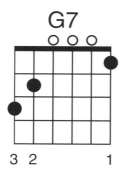

3 2   1

C7

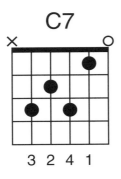

x   o

3 2 4 1

B7

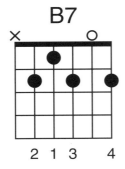

x   o

2 1 3   4

6th-String Barre Form

1 3 1 2 1 1

5th-String Barre Form

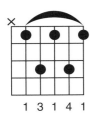

x

1 3 1 4 1

If you play the 6th-string form with your first finger on the third fret, you have a G7 chord.

G7

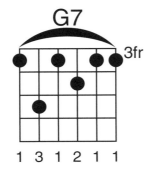

3fr

1 3 1 2 1 1

If you play the 5th-string form with your first finger on the third fret, you have a C7 chord.

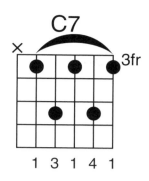

Now let's incorporate dominant seventh chords into some chord progressions. For this first example, use all barre chords. (Again, refer to the Appendix if you can't remember the notes on the 6th and 5th strings.)

Example 27

This example is played with all open forms.

Example 28

And here's a 12-bar blues in the key of A. In the blues, it's common to use all dominant seventh chords. Use barre forms for the A7 and D7 and an open E7 chord.

Example 29

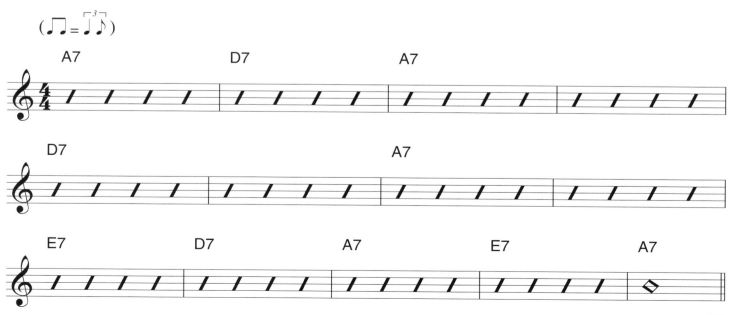

Minor Seventh Chords

Minor seventh chords sound a little more sophisticated or jazzy than minor chords. They're usually inter-changeable with minor chords (triads), so experiment with them to hear the different effect they create.

Open Forms

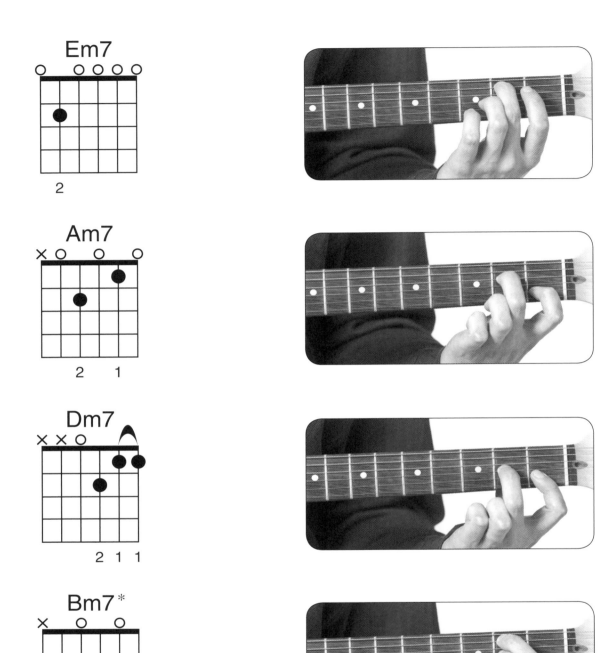

Em7

2

Am7

2 1

Dm7

2 1 1

Bm7 *

2 3 4

*This open Bm7 form is used much less frequently than the open B7 form.

Notice that these forms differ from the dominant forms by one note only. The 3rd of each dominant chord is lowered to create a minor seventh chord. (Cm7 doesn't appear as an open form because the 3rd of C7, E, is lowered to E♭, which is not an open string.)

6th-String Barre Form

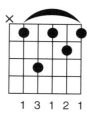

1 3 1 1 1

5th-String Barre Form

1 3 1 2 1

If you play the 6th-string form with your first finger on the third fret, you have a Gm7 chord.

Gm7

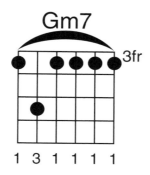

3fr

1 3 1 1 1 1

If you play the 5th-string form with your first finger on the third fret, you have a Cm7 chord.

Cm7

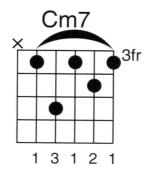

3fr

1 3 1 2 1

Let's incorporate minor seventh chords into some progressions. This first one uses all open forms.

Example 30

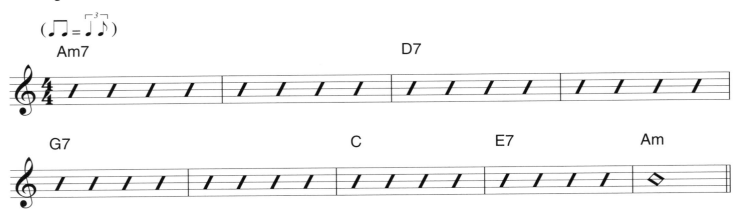

For this example, use barre chords throughout, referencing the neck diagram in the Appendix if necessary.

Example 31

This next example is a 12-bar minor blues in the key of A. In a minor blues, it's common to use all minor seventh and dominant seventh chords. We'll use all barre forms in this one.

Example 32

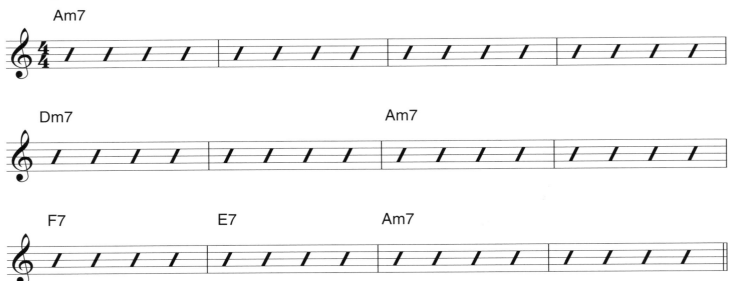

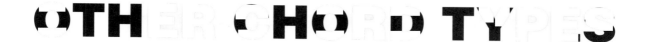

Besides power chords, triads, and seventh chords, there are others that occur often as well. Let's learn a few of these.

Suspended Chords

Suspended chords are similar to power chords in that they don't have a 3rd. However, they are still three-note chords; the 3rd is simply replaced by either a 2nd or a 4th. The former results in a sus2 chord (1–2–5), and the latter results in a sus4 chord (1–4–5).

Open Forms

Esus4

2 3 4

Asus2

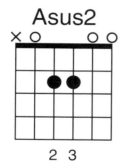

2 3

Asus4

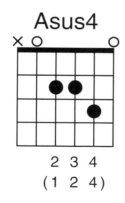

2 3 4
(1 2 4)

Dsus2

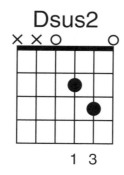

1 3

Dsus4

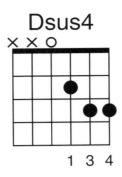

× × O

1 3 4

6th-String Barre Form

suspended 4th

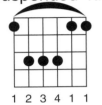

1 2 3 4 1 1

If you play the 6th-string form with your first finger on the third fret, you have a Gsus4 chord.

Gsus4

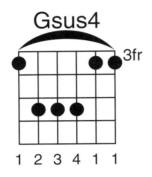

3fr

1 2 3 4 1 1

Suspended 2nd barre chords based off a 6th-string root aren't typically used.

5th-String Barre Forms

suspended 4th

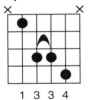

× ×

1 3 3 4

suspended 2nd

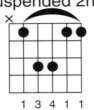

×

1 3 4 1 1

If you play the 5th-string form with your first finger on the third fret, you have a Csus4 chord and a Csus2 chord.

Csus4

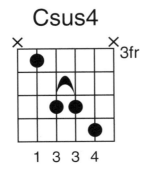

× ×3fr

1 3 3 4

Csus2

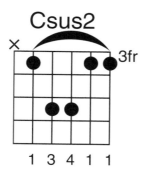

×   3fr

1   3   4   1   1

Suspended chords are often (though not always) interchangeable with their major and minor counterparts. They also often resolve to (are followed by) their major or minor counterparts. For example, Dsus2 or Dsus4 will often be followed by D (or Dm).

Add Nine Chords

Add nine chords (add9) have a lush quality that can be just what's needed to give an extra lift to a chord progression. They can either be major (1–3–5–9) or minor (1–♭3–5–9). (The 9th interval is the same as the 2nd, only an octave higher.) Add nine chords are generally interchangeable with major or minor chords.

Open Forms

Eadd9

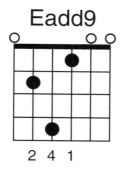

○   ○ ○

2   4   1

Em(add9)

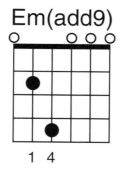

○   ○ ○ ○

1   4

Aadd9

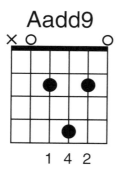

× ○   ○

1   4   2

Am(add9)

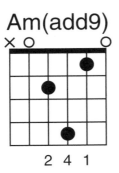

6th-String Barre Forms

major add9

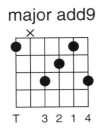

T 3 2 1 4

minor add9

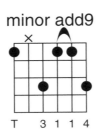

T 3 1 1 4

The thumb (indicated by "T") is optional in these forms. You can also just play the top four strings.

If you play the 6th-string forms with your thumb on the third fret, you have Gadd9 and Gm(add9) chords.

Gadd9

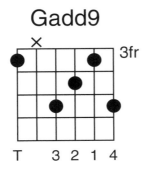

3fr

T 3 2 1 4

Gm(add9)

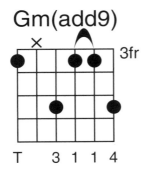

3fr

T 3 1 1 4

Barre forms of add9 chords based off a 5th-string root aren't typically used.

Now let's play a few full songs that make use of everything we've covered. The DVD will show you which chord forms are used, but feel free to experiment with your own choices for a different sound.

Example 33

This is a mid-tempo shuffle groove in E minor with a lot of chord changes.

Repeat and fade

Example 34

Here's a hard rockin' tune in the key of G. There are lots of power chords and suspended chords in this one.

Example 35

This final example is a mid-tempo rocker in the key of A.

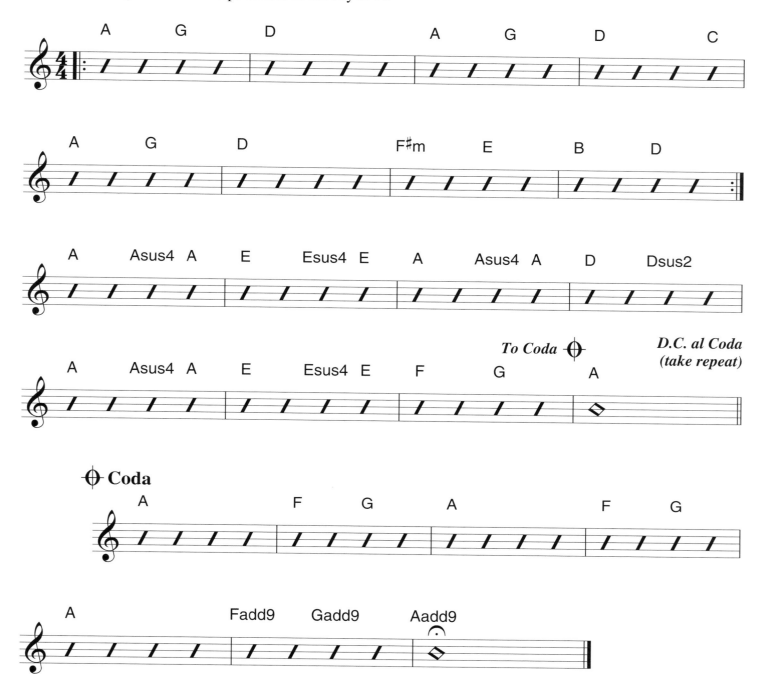

Appendix

Neck Diagram

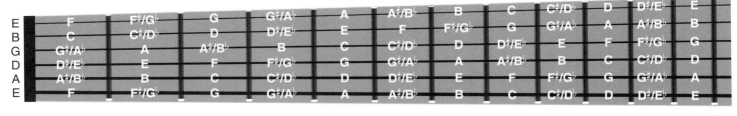

frets: *3*   *5*   *7*   *9*   *12*

Twelve Major Scales

C Major: C–D–E–F–G–A–B

G Major: G–A–B–C–D–E–F♯

D Major: D–E–F♯–G–A–B–C♯

A Major: A–B–C♯–D–E–F♯–G♯

E Major: E–F♯–G♯–A–B–C♯–D♯

B Major: B–C♯–D♯–E–F♯–G♯–A♯

F Major: F–G–A–B♭–C–D–E

B♭ Major: B♭–C–D–E♭–F–G–A

E♭ Major: E♭–F–G–A♭–B♭–C–D

A♭ Major: A♭–B♭–C–D♭–E♭–F–G

D♭ Major: D♭–E♭–F–G♭–A♭–B♭–C

G♭ Major: G♭–A♭–B♭–C♭–D♭–E♭–F

Recommended Listening

Power Chords

"Rock You Like a Hurricane" – Scorpions

"Welcome to the Jungle" – Guns N' Roses

"Smells Like Teen Spirit" – Nirvana

Open Chords

"Back in Black" – AC/DC

"Paradise City" – Guns N' Roses

"American Girl" – Tom Petty

Barre Chords

"Say It Ain't So" – Weezer

"You Really Got Me" – The Kinks

"Flake" – Jack Johnson

Seventh Chords

"Born on the Bayou" – Creedence Clearwater Revival

"Taxman" – The Beatles

"Fifty Ways to Leave Your Lover" – Paul Simon

Suspended Chords

"Behind Blue Eyes," "Pinball Wizard" – The Who

"Three Libras" – A Perfect Circle

"Don't Dream It's Over" – Crowded House

"What I Am" – Edie Brickell and New Bohemians